To Lauren,

Your sense of curiosity and quest
to be the best in everything you
do is a daily inspiration!

– *Cheryl Johnson*

2022

This book is given with love

To:

Cecilia Arco

From:

Aunt Shirley & Uncle Jim

Happy Birthday

Hello There!

Did you know that birds come in all shapes, sizes, colors, and are all around us? Look up, look down, look all around, and chances are you'll see some birds! Let's go on a birding scavenger hunt and search for birds in all the different habitats they live in around the United States.

As you fill out these activity pages, look for clues in the pictures of the birds:

 Can you tell the type of habitat from the **background of the photo**?

 The **bird's bill** is another good place to look for clues because it will help you decide what that bird might eat.

- **A long, pointed bill** is perfect for spearing fish.
- **A hooked bill** is perfect for tearing meat into bite-size pieces.
- **A small, pointed bill** on a little bird is a great tool for capturing insects hiding in small places.
- **A cone-shaped bill** is just what you need to eat seeds and/or plants.

 The **size of the bird** can also help you figure out what it eats. A small bird certainly can't eat a big fish. But remember, sometimes big birds eat little things

 Also, a **bird's name** can sometimes tell you a lot about it, like what type of habitat it lives in or what it likes to eat.

If you're stuck on a question, a good place to help you on your adventure is by visiting the website **www.AllAboutBirds.org**. Here, you can discover all kinds of interesting information about birds. Once you're done filling out your answers, you can check the answer key at the back of the book.

Good luck and have fun,
Cheryl Johnson

Birding Terms

Foraging

Foraging means the bird is searching for something to eat such as seeds, insects, or small animals. A bird that eats a little bit of everything is called an "omnivore."

Habitat

A "habitat" is the physical surroundings where the bird lives. Habitats are made up of several physical factors, such as the type of plants that are around or if there's water in the area.

Migration

"Migration" refers to the regular movement of birds from one location to another. Migration often happens during different seasons. For example, some birds spend their winters in South America, and in the spring and summer they move to the United States to start their family. Birds can travel hundreds - or even thousands - of miles and fly over entire oceans during their seasonal migration.

☐ Where birds can be found
☐ Where birds *cannot* be found

Want to Learn More About Birds?

Merlin Phone App:

Identify a bird with a photo, or if you don't have a photo, it will ask you 5 simple questions to help you figure out what the bird is.

Websites:

www.AllAboutBirds.org

www.ebird.org

www.FeederWatch.org

American Kestrel

These birds, like many birds, migrate, so depending on the time of year,
you can probably see an American Kestrel where you live. They are aggressive hunters
and if you look closely at its bill you might discover some clues about what
this bird likes to eat. Does the picture give you any clues to help you figure out where
this bird lives? Where do you think you might see a post out in the open?

Fun Facts

In the United States, the American Kestrel is the smallest and most common member of the falcon family of birds. American Kestrels can see ultraviolet light, which allows them to see where their prey urinate (go to the bathroom) and leave a urination trail. They can follow this trail and use it to catch food. Can you think of any creatures that might be large enough to leave a urine trail as they move around?

Height
10 Inches = iPad

Weight
4.1 Ounces = Toothpaste

Location
Fall + Winter   Spring + Summer

What Do These Birds Primarily Eat?

Crustaceans   Fish & Amphibians   Insects   Fruit   Plants

Small Animals   Mollusks & Clams   Seeds   All of the Above

What Habitat Will You Find These Birds In?

Beaches & Coastlines   Bushes & Shrubs   Trees & Forests

Swamps & Marshes   Fields & Meadows   Lakes & Ponds

Can You See American Kestrels Where You Live?

Yes, I can see them   No, they aren't where I live

American Oystercatcher

This pretty bird with the bright orange bill is an American Oystercatcher.
It's a medium-size bird whose name will tell you a lot about what their favorite food is.
They nest on open sand or on shell or gravel ridges in salt marshes. You can figure out
this bird's habitat by looking at the photograph of where the bird is standing,
and then compare it with the map of where the bird lives.

Fun Facts

American Oystercatchers are the only birds in their habitat that can open up mussels and other creatures with shells. They do it by inserting their sharp bills between the shell halves and biting the muscles that keep the two sides of the shells closed. Originally called the "sea pie," these birds were renamed after they were observed eating oysters.

Height
17 Inches = Blender

Weight
1.4 Pounds = Basketball

Location
All Year

What Do These Birds Primarily Eat?

Crustaceans   Fish & Amphibians   Insects   Fruit   Plants

Small Animals   Mollusks & Clams   Seeds   All of the Above

What Habitat Will You Find These Birds In?

Beaches & Coastlines   Bushes & Shrubs   Trees & Forests

Swamps & Marshes   Fields & Meadows   Lakes & Ponds

Can You See American Oystercatchers Where You Live?

Yes, I can see them   No, they aren't where I live

Black & White Warbler

These cute little birds are just a bundle of energy, zipping up and down tree branches as they look for food. It's easy to tell this bird's favorite food from this picture! If you think about what this bird is eating and where the bird might be able to find the type of creature, I bet you can figure out what habitat this bird lives in. What the bird is standing on will also give you some clues.

Fun Facts

On the way from their winter home in South America to their summer home in the United States, Black & White Warblers - along with other warblers - will fly hundreds of miles all night from Mexico to Texas; right over the Gulf of Mexico. They have to eat lots and lots of food before they leave so they have enough energy to fly all those miles.

Height

5 Inches = iPhone

Weight

0.4 Ounces = 2 Quarters

Location

Fall + Winter   Spring + Summer

What Do These Birds Primarily Eat?

Crustaceans   Fish & Amphibians   Insects   Fruit   Plants

Small Animals   Mollusks & Clams   Seeds   All of the Above

What Habitat Will You Find These Birds In?

Beaches & Coastlines   Bushes & Shrubs   Trees & Forests

Swamps & Marshes   Fields & Meadows   Lakes & Ponds

Can You See Black & White Warblers Where You Live?

Yes, I can see them   No, they aren't where I live

Burrowing Owl

The Burrowing Owl is one of the smallest owls found in the United States. Unlike most owls, who are more comfortable in trees, Burrowing Owls live on the ground. These owls migrate and likes habitats that are warm and dry. Burrowing Owls like other owls, have bills that are hooked and sharp. Can you think of what type of food it might eat with a bill shaped like this?

Fun Facts

Burrowing Owls are one of the few types of owls that are active during the day. Most other owls are active only at night. True to their name, these owls will often make their homes in rock crevices, holes made by mammals such as squirrels and prairie dogs, and even drainage pipes. Prairie dogs live in burrows under the ground in open spaces. Does this give you a hint what habitat you might find a Burrowing Owl?

Height
8 Inches = Banana

Weight
5 Ounces = Baseball

Location
Fall + Winter   Spring + Summer

What Do These Birds Primarily Eat?

Crustaceans   Fish & Amphibians   Insects   Fruit   Plants

Small Animals   Mollusks & Clams   Seeds   All of the Above

What Habitat Will You Find These Birds In?

Beaches & Coastlines   Bushes & Shrubs   Trees & Forests

Swamps & Marshes   Fields & Meadows   Lakes & Ponds

Can You See Burrowing Owls Where You Live?

Yes, I can see them   No, they aren't where I live

Common Gallinule

This bird has a funny name and even funnier feet, but those feet are perfect for the habitat it lives in. Their feed are long and well-suited for walking in squishy mud and water. Even though Common Gallinules don't have webbed feed like ducks, they are very good swimmers. Their feet are also good for helping them to walk on top of floating plants like lily pads. Another name for them is "swamp chicken."

Fun Facts

When looking for food, Common Gallinules will use their feet to flip over leaves and see what tasty morsel might be crawling underneath. They also makes sure to eat plenty of snails and greens both in and out of the water. The Common Gallinule's bill is small and pointy. What type of food would a small and pointy bill help the Common Gallinule catch and eat?

Height
13 Inches = Hammer

Weight
14 Ounces = Soccer Ball

Location
Fall + Winter   Spring + Summer

What Do These Birds Primarily Eat?

Crustaceans   Fish & Amphibians   Insects   Fruit   Plants

Small Animals   Mollusks & Clams   Seeds   All of the Above

What Habitat Will You Find These Birds In?

Beaches & Coastlines   Bushes & Shrubs   Trees & Forests

Swamps & Marshes   Fields & Meadows   Lakes & Ponds

Can You See Common Gallinules Where You Live?

Yes, I can see them   No, they aren't where I live

Gray Catbird

Gray Catbirds are shy birds that will quickly dash out from under bushes, look for something to eat, and dash back under the bushes for safety. They will often look for food on the ground and use their long, pointy bills to move leaves aside. Can you think of what they might be looking for under leaves? Does this give you any clues about what they eat or what habitat they live in?

Fun Facts

Many birds get their names because of the sounds they make, like the Gray Catbird. The Gray Catbird is a mimic. That means it will copy the sounds that other birds, creatures, and even people make. Birds that are mimics are also known as "mockingbirds." One of the most popular calls that a Gray Catbird makes sounds just like a cat "meowing." When they start singing, their song can last up to 10 minutes.

Height

Inches = Drinking Straw

Weight

1.6 Ounces = Golf Ball

Location

Fall + Winter   Spring + Summer

What Do These Birds Primarily Eat?

Crustaceans	Fish & Amphibians	Insects	Fruit	Plants
Small Animals	Mollusks & Clams	Seeds	All of the Above	

What Habitat Will You Find These Birds In?

Beaches & Coastlines	Bushes & Shrubs	Trees & Forests
Swamps & Marshes	Fields & Meadows	Lakes & Ponds

Can You See Gray Catbirds Where You Live?

Yes, I can see them   No, they aren't where I live

Laughing Gull

This is definitely a bird that just makes you want to laugh just by looking at it. Laughing Gulls are very common and, chances are, if you live near its habitat you've probably seen one. If you are visiting their habitat, be careful about leaving any food out in the open, they're not picky eaters and might swoop down to try and steal a bite. This should give you a clue as to what they like to eat.

Fun Facts

Based on its name, can you guess how the Laughing Gull got it's name?
If you've ever see one, listen and you'll notice that it's call sounds just like someone
laughing. Ha ha ha! You might have also heard someone call a Laughing Gull a
"Sea Gull" even though Laughing Gulls don't live exclusively near the sea.
Does that give you any clues about what its habitat is?

Height
17 Inches = Blender

Weight
12 Ounces = Soup Can

Location
All Year

What Do These Birds Primarily Eat?

Crustaceans   Fish & Amphibians   Insects   Fruit   Plants

Small Animals   Mollusks & Clams   Seeds   All of the Above

What Habitat Will You Find These Birds In?

Beaches & Coastlines   Bushes & Shrubs   Trees & Forests

Swamps & Marshes   Fields & Meadows   Lakes & Ponds

Can You See Laughing Gulls Where You Live?

Yes, I can see them   No, they aren't where I live

Least Bittern

Look at the picture closely for clues on what this bird's habitat is and what it might eat. Did you notice the long legs and toes on the Least Bittern? Do these legs remind you of another bird you've read about in this book? If you guessed the Common Gallinule, you'd be right! However, unlike the Common Gallinule, it has a long and pointy beak. What food do birds with beaks like that likely eat?

Fun Facts

If a Least Bittern becomes nervous or afraid, it will freeze where it is, point its long bill to the sky, and start to sway back and forth with the reeds to helps it to blend into it surroundings. All the while, it's keeping its eyes looking towards the source of its concern in case it needs to climb deeper into the reeds. Its striped feathers (also known as plumage) match the colors of its habitat, which helps it to hide from predators.

Height

12 Inches = Soda Bottle

Weight

3.5 Ounces = Deck of Cards

Location

Fall + Winter   Spring + Summer

What Do These Birds Primarily Eat?

Crustaceans   Fish & Amphibians   Insects   Fruit   Plants

Small Animals   Mollusks & Clams   Seeds   All of the Above

What Habitat Will You Find These Birds In?

Beaches & Coastlines   Bushes & Shrubs   Trees & Forests

Swamps & Marshes   Fields & Meadows   Lakes & Ponds

Can You See Least Bitterns Where You Live?

Yes, I can see them   No, they aren't where I live

Marsh Wren

Sometimes you can figure out a lot about a creature from its name. Use this clue to help you determine what habitat you will find the Marsh Wren in. Also, look at the shape of its bill for clues about what this little bird likes to eat. It's small, narrow, and pointy, which will help it find food that might be hiding in little nooks and crevices. Can you think of anything that might want to hide from the Marsh Wren's bill?

Fun Facts

These little birds have a reputation for being very shy, and often you will only hear them rather than see them. Plus, their feathers (plumage) help them to blend into their habitat, making it even harder to see them! Even through Marsh Wrens are small and shy, they are very tough. They will fiercely guard their territory and fight off other birds that get too close to their nests, especially in the spring when they have babies to protect.

Height
5 Inches = iPhone

Weight
0.4 Ounces = 2 Quarters

Location
Fall + Winter   Spring + Summer

What Do These Birds Primarily Eat?

Crustaceans   Fish & Amphibians   Insects   Fruit   Plants

Small Animals   Mollusks & Clams   Seeds   All of the Above

What Habitat Will You Find These Birds In?

Beaches & Coastlines   Bushes & Shrubs   Trees & Forests

Swamps & Marshes   Fields & Meadows   Lakes & Ponds

Can You See Marsh Wrens Where You Live?

Yes, I can see them   No, they aren't where I live

Northern Bobwhite

This is a picture of a male and female Northern Bobwhite. As you study the photo looking for clues about their habitat and favorite food, you'll see that their feathers have different colors. Many species of birds are this way. Sometimes the male looks completely different than the female. The color of the Northern Bobwhite's feathers help them to blend into their environment and keep them safe from predators.

Fun Facts

Like other birds, the Northern Bobwhite gets its name from its whistling call. When they call out to other birds it sounds like they're saying "bobwhite, bobwhite!" These birds prefer to spend their time on the ground and will often run away when scared rather than fly. Look at their cone-shaped bill. Can you think of what type of food they might find on the ground and what that cone-shaped bill will help them eat?

Height
9 Inches = Vase

Weight
5 Ounces = Baseball

Location
All Year

What Do These Birds Primarily Eat?

Crustaceans   Fish & Amphibians   Insects   Fruit   Plants

Small Animals   Mollusks & Clams   Seeds   All of the Above

What Habitat Will You Find These Birds In?

Beaches & Coastlines   Bushes & Shrubs   Trees & Forests

Swamps & Marshes   Fields & Meadows   Lakes & Ponds

Can You See Northern Bobwhites Where You Live?

Yes, I can see them   No, they aren't where I live

Osprey

Ospreys are very good hunters with great eyesight. They will circle high in the air looking for food, and when they spot it, will dive into the water to catch their prey. This is a very good clue as to what they eat. You can also look at this Osprey's hooked bill for another clue about their favorite food. Can you guess what their habitat is based on the type of food they eat?

Fun Facts

The Osprey, like other birds, has four toes but, unlike other birds, its outer toe can turn different directions. It can grab its prey with three toes forward and one toe back or with two toes forward and two toes back. Four toes with very sharp claws and a reversible toe helps the Osprey to hold on to its food when it's flying, which is very helpful when it's trying to hold on to its slippery, wiggling prey.

Height
2 Inches = Tennis Racket

Weight
2.5 Pound = 2 Slice Toaster

Location
Fall + Winter   Spring + Summer

What Do These Birds Primarily Eat?

Crustaceans   Fish & Amphibians   Insects   Fruit   Plants

Small Animals   Mollusks & Clams   Seeds   All of the Above

What Habitat Will You Find These Birds In?

Beaches & Coastlines   Bushes & Shrubs   Trees & Forests

Swamps & Marshes   Fields & Meadows   Lakes & Ponds

Can You See Osprey Where You Live?

Yes, I can see them   No, they aren't where I live

Ring-Necked Duck

Ring-Necked Ducks are part of a group of ducks called "diving ducks." These ducks get that name because they dive under the water looking for food. They will push themselves up in the air and dive into the water, using their webbed feet to help them swim deep into the water looking for something to eat. Can you think of what type of food might be at the bottom of a pond or lake?

Fun Facts

Ring-Necked Ducks get their name from the brown ring around their neck, but this ring isn't always easy to see when the duck is swimming around. A better way to help you tell this duck apart from other ducks is by the white ring around its bill and the black tip at the end. Some people think a better name for this bird would be "Ring-Billed Duck." What do you think?

Height
17 Inches = Blender

Weight
1.4 Pound = Basketball

Location
Fall + Winter   Spring + Summer

What Do These Birds Primarily Eat?

Crustaceans   Fish & Amphibians   Insects   Fruit   Plants

Small Animals   Mollusks & Clams   Seeds   All of the Above

What Habitat Will You Find These Birds In?

Beaches & Coastlines   Bushes & Shrubs   Trees & Forests

Swamps & Marshes   Fields & Meadows   Lakes & Ponds

Can You See Ring-Necked Ducks Where You Live?

Yes, I can see them   No, they aren't where I live

Ruby-Crowned Kinglet

What these little birds lack in size, they make up for in energy! If you want to see one, you have to pay close attention because they move fast! This bird likes to move around with other birds so, if you see one, there's probably more birds close by. When birds travel together in groups like this it is called "flocking," and helps them to stay safe from predators.

Fun Facts

Ruby-Crowned Kinglets are tiny bird with lots of energy and attitude. Normally, you can't see the bright, ruby-colored feathers on the top of their head because they keep them tucked and hidden as they zip from tree to tree looking for creepy-crawly food. However, when they get mad or excited, those feathers pop up and it looks like its head is literally exploding with color!

Height

4 Inches = Softball

Weight

0.2 Ounces = Quarter

Location

Fall + Winter   Spring + Summer

What Do These Birds Primarily Eat?

Crustaceans   Fish & Amphibians   Insects   Fruit   Plants

Small Animals   Mollusks & Clams   Seeds   All of the Above

What Habitat Will You Find These Birds In?

Beaches & Coastlines   Bushes & Shrubs   Trees & Forests

Swamps & Marshes   Fields & Meadows   Lakes & Ponds

Can You See Ruby-Crowned Kinglets Where You Live?

Yes, I can see them   No, they aren't where I live

Sanderling

These cute little birds are just a bundle of energy and can be found quickly zipping up, down, and all around their habitat. They are very common throughout the United States and can be found in many states, but only in one specific habitat. Look closely at the photo for clues on what that habitat is. The bird's long bill might also give you some clues as to what its favorite food is too.

Fun Facts

Sanderlings look like completely different birds in the fall than they do in the spring. In the fall, their feathers are mostly white with light grey on their backs and heads, and in the spring they look like the bird in this photo, with speckled tan, black, and white feathers. When a bird's feathers change color in the spring, it is called their "breeding plumage" and helps them attract a mate.

Height
7 Inches = Fork

Weight
3 Ounces = Deck of Cards

Location
Fall + Winter   Spring + Summer

What Do These Birds Primarily Eat?

Crustaceans	Fish & Amphibians	Insects	Fruit	Plants
Small Animals	Mollusks & Clams	Seeds	All of the Above	

What Habitat Will You Find These Birds In?

Beaches & Coastlines	Bushes & Shrubs	Trees & Forests
Swamps & Marshes	Fields & Meadows	Lakes & Ponds

Can You See Sanderlings Where You Live?

Yes, I can see them   No, they aren't where I live

Sandhill Crane

This photo has a clue about the Sandhill Crane's habitat, but sometimes photos don't tell the whole tale. They can be found in a completely different habitats depending on the time of year, which you can see from the maps. Different habitats contain different types of food, which might give you a clue as to what they eat. Another clue is that they have something in common with Laughing Gulls. Can you guess what that is?

Fun Facts

Sandhill Cranes have a very fun courtship dance. The males and females will jump up and down, flap their wings, and bounce all over. It almost looks like they might be fighting, but they are really just trying to impress one another and attract a mate. When Sandhill Cranes choose a mate, they will stay together for their entire lives, which is uncommon since most birds choose a new mate each spring.

Height

4 Feet = Vacuum

Weight

8.6 Pounds = Gallon of Milk

Location

Fall + Winter   Spring + Summer

What Do These Birds Primarily Eat?

Crustaceans   Fish & Amphibians   Insects   Fruit   Plants

Small Animals   Mollusks & Clams   Seeds   All of the Above

What Habitat Will You Find These Birds In?

Beaches & Coastlines   Bushes & Shrubs   Trees & Forests

Swamps & Marshes   Fields & Meadows   Lakes & Ponds

Can You See Sandhill Cranes Where You Live?

Yes, I can see them   No, they aren't where I live

Spotted Towhee

The Spotted Towhee has a close cousin called the Eastern Towhee. Scientists believe that these two birds both evolved from the same species. Over time, groups of these birds became separated on different sides of North America and eventually evolved into two different species. You can tell the two species apart by the coloring on their back. Eastern Towhees have solid black feathers while Spotted Towhees have, that's right, spot

Fun Facts

This cute little bird is one of the more colorful members of the sparrow family. You can often find them in berry bushes and scratching the ground looking for food. Does this give you a clue what their habitat is, and what they might eat? Look at this short, cone-shaped bill for clues about what it might like to eat. Here's another hint: they primarily eat three of the choices below.

Height
7 Inches = Fork

Weight
1.6 Ounces = Golf Ball

Location
Fall + Winter   Spring + Summer

What Do These Birds Primarily Eat?

Crustaceans   Fish & Amphibians   Insects   Fruit   Plants

Small Animals   Mollusks & Clams   Seeds   All of the Above

What Habitat Will You Find These Birds In?

Beaches & Coastlines   Bushes & Shrubs   Trees & Forests

Swamps & Marshes   Fields & Meadows   Lakes & Ponds

Can You See Spotted Towhees Where You Live?

Yes, I can see them   No, they aren't where I live

White-Eyed Vireo

The White-Eyed Vireo is a shy little bird with a great big voice! If you happen to go out looking for them, chances are that you'll hear them way before you see them. Think about how big they are. Their small size makes it impossible to eat big things like fish and small animals. Look at their narrow and pointy bill. That bill helps them to reach in nooks and crannies when searching for food.

Fun Facts

The White-Eyed Vireo is one of only two species of "perching birds" (birds that like to stand on branches) that have white eyes and can be found in North America. When born, the eyes of the baby White-Eyed Vireos are brown, and as they get older, their eyes turn white like their parents. Can you think of what type of habitat has lots of branches and leaves for the White-Eyed Vireos to hide in?

Height
5 Inches = iPhone

Weight
0.4 Ounces = 2 Quarters

Location
Fall + Winter   Spring + Summer

What Do These Birds Primarily Eat?

Crustaceans   Fish & Amphibians   Insects   Fruit   Plants

Small Animals   Mollusks & Clams   Seeds   All of the Above

What Habitat Will You Find These Birds In?

Beaches & Coastlines   Bushes & Shrubs   Trees & Forests

Swamps & Marshes   Fields & Meadows   Lakes & Ponds

Can You See White-Eyed Vireos Where You Live?

Yes, I can see them   No, they aren't where I live

About the Author

Cheryl Johnson started on her "birding" journey in 2016. She has had a wonderful time learning about nature, discovering the incredible beauty that surrounds us, meeting lots of other fellow enthusiasts, and developing her skills and knowledge as a photographer and naturalist.

She stumbled upon wildlife photography by chance when she joined a bird walk through a local park as part of a magazine story she was writing and instantly fell in love with it! So, she grabbed her camera and prepared to take some "award-winning" photos of our fine, feathered friends because, really, how difficult could photographing birds really be? She soon discovered the answer - incredibly difficult! Not to be bested by the tiny, feathered creatures, she decided to figure out how it was done, and an obsession was born!

Cheryl started by purchasing feeders and photographing the birds visiting her backyard and soon found herself wandering all over town, up and down beaches, through forests, and all over the state snapping pictures of everything that flew past her lens.

Cheryl's award-winning photography has been featured in several publications, marketing campaigns, and websites. Her art has been displayed in several businesses: The Five Points Museum of Contemporary Art and the Victoria Art League in Victoria, Texas. She's also been a guest speaker sharing her passion with many groups and organizations. When not traveling all over the state, country, and world photographing birds and other wildlife, she lives in Victoria, Texas, with her husband, two daughters, and her dog.

Junior Ornithologist

Having completed the necessary course study,

this is to certify that

_____

is an official Junior Ornithologist.

"May birds of a feather stick together!"

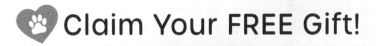

🐾 Claim Your FREE Gift!

Visit ➡ PDICBooks.com/Gift

Thank you for purchasing My Bird Scavenger Hunt,
and welcome to the Puppy Dogs & Ice Cream family.

We're certain you're going to love the little gift
we've prepared for you at the website above.

Answer Key

Type of Bird	Eat	Habitat
American Kestrel	Small Animals	Fields & Meadows
American Oystercatcher	Mollusks & Clams	Beaches & Coastlines
Black & White Warbler	Insects	Trees & Forests
Burrowing Owl	Small Animals	Fields & Meadows
Common Gallinule	Plants, Mollusks & Clams, Insects, and Seeds	Swamps & Marshes
Gray Catbird	Insects	Bushes & Shrubs
Laughing Gull	All of the Above	Beaches & Coastlines
Least Bittern	Fish & Amphibians	Swamps & Marshes
Marsh Wren	Insects	Swamps & Marshes
Northern Bobwhite	Plants and Seeds	Fields & Meadows
Osprey	Fish & Amphibians	Lakes & Ponds
Ringed-Neck Duck	Plants	Lakes & Ponds
Ruby-Crowned Kinglet	Insects	Trees & Forests
Sanderling	Mollusks & Clams	Beaches & Coastlines
Sandhill Crane	All of the Above	Swamps & Marshes and Fields & Meadows
Spotted Towhee	Fruit, Insects, and Seeds	Bushes & Shrubs
White-Eyed Vireo	Insects	Bushes & Shrubs

CPSIA information can be obtained
at www.ICGtesting.com
Printed in the USA
LVHW071716140522
718797LV00007B/174

9 781956 462883